The Daughter Behind the Mask

Break Free from False Identity, Heal from Hidden Wounds, and Walk Boldly in Who God Created You to Be

Sabrina Gray

Dedication

To my husband Phillip Gray Jr, who has walked with me through every phase of my becoming. For over a decade, you have loved me through every version of myself—through the highs, the breaking, the healing, and the rebuilding. It is no small thing to stand beside someone who is constantly growing and changing, yet you have remained a steady presence, a constant source of love, patience, and encouragement. Thank you for giving me the space to grow while always reminding me of who I was called to be.

To every woman who, at some point, poured into me—whether through a conversation, a prayer, a moment of encouragement, or simply by living in a way that showed me what was possible. Some of you were in my life for a season, others for a lifetime, but all of you left something with me. While no one but God could truly lead me to this place of freedom, I honor the ways He used you to remind me of who I was becoming.

And to the woman who is in the middle—the one who feels stuck between who she was and who she is becoming. The one who feels unseen, exhausted, and unsure if real change is even possible.

This book is for you.

For the woman who has tried everything in her own strength but still feels like she's running in circles, hitting the same walls, fighting the same battles.

You are not crazy. You are not forgotten. You are not beyond restoration.

There is freedom, healing, and wholeness on the other side of this. My prayer is that these pages help you step fully into the life you were always meant to live—not in striving, but in surrender. Not in performance, but in purpose.

Because God never called you to live bound.

You were created for more.

And it's time to finally walk in it

Contents

Introduction 1

Chapter 1: Recognizing Your Prototype..7

Chapter 2: The God Who Sees The Real You 21

Chapter 3: The Pressing Process 37

Chapter 4: Sonship vs. Orphan Mentality Stepping Into Your True
Identity 57

Chapter 5: Becoming Rooted—Living As A Son/Daughter In
Everyday Life 63

Chapter 6: Breaking Free & Walking In Authority.......................69

Chapter 7: Living Free & Walking In Authority...........................75

Chapter 8: Walking In Purpose, Living From
Your True Identity 81

Chapter 9: Sealing The Shift, Walking In Unbreakable Identity.87

You Are No Longer in Process, You Are Positioned 93

Introduction

I spent my twenties as a shell of myself.

For ten years, I was what I now call a "professional chameleon." I could walk into any room and instantly become whatever version of myself I thought would be most acceptable. I built a prototype, a carefully crafted model of who I believed I needed to be in order to feel loved, accepted, and safe.

This wasn't the kind of prototype engineers build before mass production. This was a version of myself pieced together from the qualities of women I admired. I would think, "I love the way she mothers her children," or "I love how she carries herself as a wife," or "I love how she runs her business." Notch by notch, I built what I thought a beautiful, successful woman of God was supposed to be.

The problem was, that woman wasn't me.

I didn't realize that with every shift and adaptation, I was slowly dying inside. The very qualities I tried to suppress were the ones God had intentionally placed in me. They were designed for a purpose, meant to solve specific problems and fulfill a calling only I could fulfill.

This book is about my journey from living as that prototype to discovering the freedom of being exactly who God created me to be. But more importantly, it's about your journey. It is about recognizing where you might be living behind a mask, understanding why you created that mask in the first place, and finding the courage to step into your authentic identity in Christ.

How to Engage with This Book

This book was designed for deep transformation, not just casual reading. As you move through each chapter, you will have two ways to engage with the content:

Read It Straight Through – If you are in a season where you need to absorb the message first, you can read this book from start to finish and let the truths settle in your heart. Each chapter builds on the last, walking you through identity, freedom, and spiritual authority.

Read & Engage with Reflection Questions – For those who want a more immersive experience, take your time with each chapter. Answer the reflection questions and activations at the end. This will allow you to process, apply, and fully walk in your transformation.

A Challenge: While this book can be read individually, transformation often happens best in community. Consider reading through it with a trusted friend, mentor, or small group. Walking through this journey with someone else can bring deeper accountability, breakthrough, and encouragement. But whether you read alone or with others, the most important thing is that you engage with it fully.

However you choose to move through this book, commit to the journey. Don't rush past what God is doing in you. This is not just another book, it is a call to step into the fullness of who you were created to be.

The Genesis of a Prototype

My story began in Texas, where I experienced brokenness at a young age. Sexual abuse at various points in my childhood left scars that were never properly addressed. I learned to move forward while the weight of those experiences lingered in the background.

When I moved to Washington state, it felt like a fresh start, even a new identity. People started calling me Gracee instead of Sabrina.

It was as if I had joined the Witness Protection Program. I had the perfect opportunity to create a new life for myself. Instead of discovering who I truly was, I started building a version of myself that I believed would be more acceptable.

I did this because I wanted to belong. I wanted to be loved. I wanted to be included. But deep down, I didn't believe that the real Sabrina, with all her quirks, her loudness, her intensity, and her past—was enough.

Your prototype may have formed differently. Perhaps yours came from:

- **Rejection or abandonment**. If someone significant in your life rejected you, you may have created a version of yourself you thought would be impossible to reject.
- **Cultural or societal pressure**. You may have absorbed messages about what is considered acceptable or valued and reshaped yourself to fit that image.
- **Religious expectations**. You may have tried to conform to a rigid idea of what a "good Christian" should look like.
- **Trauma**. If you have experienced pain or violation, you may have created a protective shell to prevent being hurt again.

No matter how it formed, your prototype was created for a reason. It served a purpose—to protect you, to help you belong, or to keep you safe. Understanding this is important because it allows you to extend compassion to yourself. You did not create a false self out of malice or deceit but out of a genuine need to survive and belong.

The Cost of Living Behind a Mask

While my prototype may have felt safe, it came at a tremendous cost.

Emotionally, I was exhausted. Performing, hiding, and pretending are all draining. A lie is always harder to maintain than the truth. Anxiety, stress, and creative blocks followed because I was not operating from the authentic way God had wired me.

Relationally, my connections remained surface-level. The people in my life were not getting to know the real me. They were getting to know my representative, as one of my mentors called it.

Spiritually, I was disconnected from God's truth about my identity. By crafting my own narrative of who I needed to be, I was, in effect, telling God that His creation was not good enough.

This way of living made it harder for me to be a mother, a friend, and a wife. It made it harder for me to show up fully in any space because I was constantly filtering myself through the prototype I had created.

Perhaps you can relate. Perhaps you have felt the weight of trying to be someone you are not, the loneliness of not being truly known, or the spiritual emptiness that comes from disconnecting from God's design for your life.

The Journey to Authenticity

My journey toward dismantling my prototype began when I became tired. Tired of performing. Tired of hiding. Tired of pretending.

I remember being on a prayer call when someone told me, "You have to grieve the old version of yourself." That statement struck me deeply. I needed to grieve the ways I had made myself more "digestible," all the ways I tried to be what I was not, and all the ways I had silenced myself in order to maintain relationships.

CHAPTER 1

Recognizing Your Prototype

T here is a profound difference between who God created you to be and who you have learned to be.

The journey of faith isn't just about salvation. It is about restoration: a return to the authentic identity that God designed for you before the foundation of the world. But for many of us, that journey is complicated by what I call "the prototype," a carefully crafted version of ourselves that we have built to feel safe, accepted, and loved in a broken world.

Before we go further, let's pause and consider what Scripture tells us in 2 Corinthians 5:17:

"Therefore, if anyone is in Christ, the new creation has come: The old has gone, the new is here!"

This verse isn't just about the moment of salvation. It speaks to an ongoing transformation, a stripping away of the old self we have constructed and an embracing of the new self that God intended.

This chapter is about recognizing that prototype so that, with God's help, you can begin to dismantle it and embrace your true identity in Christ.

The Making of a Prototype

I remember moving to Seattle at 18, having just come to know the Lord. I was suddenly surrounded by young Christians who had been in church for years, and I felt so behind. I didn't have the same knowledge of Scripture or the same religious background. It felt like I was trying to catch up to everyone else's spiritual journey.

That move gave me an opportunity to reinvent myself. No one knew me except the family I had moved with, who even gave me a different name. Instead of Sabrina Rollins, I became Sabrina Gracie Nicole Hernandez. It was like joining the Witness Protection Program: a clean slate, a fresh start.

But instead of using that opportunity to discover who God had created me to be, I started building what I thought was a better, more acceptable version of myself. I wasn't happy with where I came from, and I wasn't proud of the fact that I had gone 18 years without truly knowing God.

Shortly after arriving, I was made a leader at church. This added another layer of pressure. I felt like I had to look the part and perform perfectly. I believed that if I could just "fake it till I make it," I would eventually become the person I was pretending to be. What I didn't realize was how much damage faking actually does to every area of life.

Your prototype may have formed differently, but the motivations are often the same.

Fear of rejection—You fear that if people see the real you, they won't accept you.

Religious expectations—You feel pressure to conform to a set of behaviors that define what a "good Christian" should look like.

Comparison—You measure yourself against others and feel like you don't measure up.

Past trauma—You created a protective shell to prevent being hurt again.

Performance culture—You believe your worth is tied to what you accomplish.

New beginnings—Like me, you may have used a major life transition as an opportunity to create a "new you."

Whatever the origin, your prototype wasn't created out of malice. It came from a genuine desire to belong, to be accepted, and to survive in environments that felt threatening to your true self.

The problem is, God knew you before He formed you in the womb. As Jeremiah 1:5 tells us, He designed you with intention and purpose. Every aspect of who you are: your personality, your gifts, and your heart, was carefully crafted by the Creator of the universe.

When we live as our prototype rather than our authentic self in Christ, we are essentially telling God, "What You created isn't good enough."

Signs You're Living as Your Prototype

How do you know if you're living as your prototype rather than your authentic self in Christ? Here are some signs I have experienced and observed.

1. You Are Constantly Performing Rather Than Abiding

The Christian life isn't about performance. It is about connection.

Jesus used the metaphor of a vine and branches in John 15 to illustrate this truth. He didn't say, "Try really hard to produce fruit." He said, "Remain in me, and you will bear fruit."

When we are living as our prototype, we focus more on doing rather than being, on earning approval rather than abiding in Christ.

For years, I performed. I could walk into any room and immediately assess who I needed to be to be accepted. I thought I was being adaptable, but in reality, I was disconnected from the vine, trying to produce fruit through my own effort.

The exhausting part? It was never enough. No matter how well I performed or how many compliments I received, I was always questioning if I was truly liked or if people only accepted the version of me I was presenting.

2. Your Identity Is in What You Do, Not in Who You Are in Christ

Our true identity is found in Christ, not in our titles, achievements, or roles.

I defined myself by what I did: wife, mom, salon owner, educator. When God called me to make changes in my life, it shook me because I realized how much of my identity was wrapped up in titles.

I wasn't just grieving the change. I was grieving the identity I had built around my roles.

I found myself asking, "Who am I without these titles?" I had to learn that my worth wasn't in what I did but in who I was in Christ.

3. You Fear People's Opinions More Than You Trust God

Proverbs 29:25 tells us, "Fear of man will prove to be a snare, but whoever trusts in the Lord is kept safe."

When we are more concerned with people's opinions than with what God says, we remain trapped in our prototype.

For years, I was terrified of rejection. I avoided conflict at all costs. If someone hurt me, I would smile and pretend it didn't bother me just to keep the peace. I would apologize even when I wasn't wrong, just to maintain relationships.

I thought I was being a peacemaker, but I was really just a people-pleaser. My relationships were surface-level because I never allowed people to see the real me: flaws and all.

4. You Present Different Versions of Yourself in Different Contexts

Integrity means being whole and undivided. When we present different versions of ourselves depending on our environment, we are living in duplicity rather than authenticity.

I was a professional chameleon. I could blend into any room, adapt to any group, and figure out how to be liked. But in doing so, I lost myself. I borrowed pieces of other people's identities because I didn't believe my own was enough.

I would see a woman who was an amazing mother and think, "I need to be like that." I would hear someone in ministry and think, "I need to sound like her." I was constantly piecing together a version of myself that I thought was more lovable and more acceptable.

The truth was, I had no idea who I really was because I had never given myself permission to discover who God created me to be.

5. You Are Emotionally Disconnected

Jesus wept. He expressed anger, compassion, and joy. He did not suppress His emotions; He expressed them authentically.

For the longest time, I was disconnected from my emotions. I could feel the weight of tears wanting to come, but I couldn't cry naturally. I had learned to guard myself: guard my words, guard my emotions, guard my heart.

It got so bad that I would put on a sad movie just to invoke tears, hoping it would release whatever was building up inside me. But even then, the tears didn't feel real because I wasn't connected to the source of my emotions.

We can only truly connect with others and with God when we allow ourselves to be emotionally present and honest.

6. You Delay Obedience Out of Fear

Obedience is the natural overflow of love for God. When we delay obedience out of fear or a desire for control, we are prioritizing our prototype's safety over our relationship with Christ.

I struggled to walk away from relationships that had become idols. God would speak clearly, showing me how these relationships had taken His place in my life, yet I hesitated to set boundaries. Not because I didn't want to obey, but because I was scared. I didn't trust that God's way was better than my understanding.

I learned that delayed obedience is still disobedience. First Samuel 15:23 tells us:

"For rebellion is like the sin of divination, and arrogance like the evil of idolatry."

When we substitute our judgment for God's, we step into rebellion: something God takes seriously.

7. You Have Made Idols of Success and People's Approval

An idol is anything we place above God in our hearts. For many of us, success and approval have become idols: things we pursue with more passion than we pursue God Himself.

I didn't realize how much I needed people's approval until God started to strip it away. I was more concerned with applause and validation than with obedience. I needed people to affirm that I was doing a good job, that I was valuable, that I was worthy.

I made success an idol because it made me feel seen. I made people's opinions an idol because they made me feel accepted. But these idols always left me empty, constantly craving more validation.

8. You Feel Unknown and Isolated Even in Community

God created us to be fully known: first by Him, then in authentic community with others. When we live as our prototype, we might be surrounded by people but still feel deeply alone.

Even when I was surrounded by love, I felt unknown. Not because people didn't care about me, but because I never allowed myself to be truly seen. I guarded my heart, protected my image, and curated a version of myself that I thought was more lovable.

I was lonely, not because I lacked community, but because I lacked authenticity. I was so busy performing that I never allowed myself to receive genuine love or connection.

The Cost of Living Behind a Mask

Jesus said, "The thief comes only to steal and kill and destroy; I have come that they may have life, and have it to the full" (John 10:10).

Satan, the thief, works tirelessly to steal the abundant life Jesus promised. One of his most effective strategies is keeping us trapped in our prototypes: exhausted by performance, disconnected from God's love, and isolated from authentic community.

At first, living behind a mask may feel like self-preservation, but in reality, it leads to deep disconnection.

When We Live as Our Prototype, We Experience:

1. Spiritual Disconnection

Our relationship with God becomes performance-based rather than love-based. Instead of resting in the truth that we are fully known and loved by Him, we strive to earn His approval or the approval of others. We may still pray, worship, and serve, but we do so from a place of fear and striving rather than intimacy.

Over time, this disconnect leaves us feeling spiritually empty, like we are constantly pouring out but never being truly filled.

2. Emotional Exhaustion

Performance is exhausting. Pretending is exhausting. Hiding is exhausting.

Living as a curated version of yourself rather than as the person God created you to be takes a toll on your mental and emotional well-being. You're constantly monitoring how you are being perceived, adjusting your words, tone, or actions to fit the expectations of those around you.

But no matter how well you perform, it never feels like enough. You still wonder:

"Would they love me if they knew the real me?"

True rest only comes when we stop performing and start abiding in the unconditional love of Christ.

3. Relational Isolation

When we wear a mask, the people who love us aren't actually loving us; they're loving the version of us we've carefully constructed.

This creates an unbearable loneliness. Even if we are surrounded by people, we still feel unknown and unseen.

God designed us for true fellowship: to be fully known, fully loved, and fully accepted. But we cannot experience authentic connection while living in hiding.

4. Purpose Limitation

God's calling on your life is not for the version of you that the world finds acceptable. It's for the real you, the one He uniquely designed.

The prototype can never fulfill the calling God has placed on your life because it was never meant to. Only your true identity in Christ can fully walk in the purpose He has for you.

Trying to fulfill your purpose while living as a false version of yourself will always lead to frustration. You'll feel like something is missing, because it is.

The good news? God is not asking you to earn His love or prove your worth. He is inviting you to rest in the identity He has already given you.

The Truth About Who You Are

As you begin to recognize your prototype, it's essential to anchor yourself in what God says about you. Your true identity isn't something you create or earn; it is given to you by God.

You are:

A child of God, loved and chosen before the foundation of the world.

A new creation in Christ, with the old gone and the new here.

God's masterpiece, created for good works that He prepared in advance for you to do.

These truths aren't just comforting statements; they are the bedrock reality of who you are. They hold more weight than any prototype you've built or any perception others have of you.

The journey of faith is about aligning your lived experience with this spiritual reality. It's about letting go of the false self you've constructed and embracing the true self God created.

Beginning the Journey of Dismantling

As you start this process, keep these three principles in mind:

1. Agree with God Quickly

When God reveals areas where you've been living inauthentically, don't resist or argue. Agree with Him about who you truly are in Christ.

This submission invites His grace into your life and accelerates your healing.

2. Give Yourself Room to Grieve

Letting go of your prototype is a process of release. It's okay to mourn the passing of something that once felt safe, even if it wasn't healthy.

Jesus said, "Blessed are those who mourn, for they will be comforted" (Matthew 5:4).

This grief isn't about regret; it's about honoring the transition and allowing God to fill the spaces where false identities once stood.

3. Lean Into God's Grace

You cannot change yourself. But God's grace empowers transformation.

You don't have to struggle through this journey alone; you can rest in His power to reshape and restore you.

The process isn't always easy, but Jesus' words remain true:

"Then you will know the truth, and the truth will set you free." (John 8:32)

As you embrace God's truth about who you are, you will find a freedom that performance and pretending could never provide.

Reflection Questions

Take a moment to reflect on what you just read. You can engage with these prompts now, or return to them later as you process this chapter.

1) When you look at your life, what do you think has shaped your prototype the most? Was it family expectations, past trauma, comparison, or something else?

2) How did your prototype help you feel safe or accepted? What did it give you that you thought you needed?

3) What moments in your life confirmed or reinforced the need for your prototype? Were there specific experiences that caused you to believe your true self wasn't enough?

4) Reflect on Jeremiah 1:5: "Before I formed you in the womb, I knew you. Before you were born, I set you apart." How does this truth challenge the identity you've built around your prototype?

5) What areas of your life do you feel afraid to surrender to God because they are tied to the version of yourself that you've created?

6) If you could live fully as your authentic self in Christ, what would that look like? How would it feel different from how you're living now?

Practical Exercise: Meeting Your Prototype

In Psalm 139:23-24, David prays:

"Search me, God, and know my heart. Test me and know my anxious thoughts. See if there is any offensive way in me, and lead me in the way everlasting."

Take some time this week to invite God into this process of self-discovery.

1 Find a quiet place to be alone with God. Read Jeremiah 1:5 aloud and ask God to reveal where your prototype was first formed.

2 In your journal, answer these questions:

- When did my prototype first develop?
- What circumstances led to its formation?
- How has it shaped the way I relate to others and to God?

3 Write a letter to your prototype.

- Acknowledge why you created it and how it helped you feel secure.
- Release it and surrender it to God, asking Him to help you step into your true identity in Christ.

Recognizing your prototype is just the first step. In the chapters ahead, we'll dive deeper into understanding God's perspective on your identity, breaking agreement with the lies that have shaped you, and stepping into the freedom of living authentically in Christ

CHAPTER 2

The God Who Sees The Real You

"You are the God who sees me."

— Genesis 16:13

In the vast desert of Shur, a woman named Hagar found herself alone, pregnant, and in despair. Fleeing mistreatment in Abraham and Sarah's household, she had nowhere to go and no one to turn to. But in that place of absolute isolation, God met her. The Creator of the universe saw her in her distress, called her by name, and spoke directly to her situation. In response to this divine encounter, Hagar gave God a name no one had used before: El Roi, "The God who sees me."

This story isn't just a historical account. It is a profound revelation of God's character, speaking directly to those of us who have spent years living behind a prototype. When we've been striving to be seen and validated by others, the truth that God already sees us, fully and completely, can be both comforting and terrifying.

The God Who Sees Beyond the Mask

What does it mean that God is El Roi, the God who sees? It means nothing about you is hidden from Him, not your struggles, fears, doubts, or dreams. He sees beyond the prototype you've created and knows the authentic person underneath.

I remember a season when I felt profoundly unseen. Despite being surrounded by people, I was deeply alone. Relationships I thought were solid had shifted, leaving me wondering if anyone truly knew or understood me. I was carrying heartbreak and grief no one else seemed to grasp, and the weight of that isolation felt unbearable.

It wasn't until I hit my lowest point that I truly encountered God as El Roi. In that dark place, I realized that even though people didn't fully see my pain, God did. He was present, seeing every tear and knowing every unspoken thought. Even when my emotions clouded my ability to feel Him, He was there, seeing me with perfect clarity.

What struck me most was that God's clearest revelation of Himself as "the One who sees" didn't come through a great blessing or mountaintop experience. It came in the wilderness, in Hagar's most desperate hour. Similarly, I discovered El Roi not in moments of triumph but in my brokenness. It was there, in that vulnerable place, that I realized I was fully known by God.

This revelation is transformative because it exposes the reason we create prototypes in the first place. We craft false versions of ourselves because we fear that if people saw the real us, with all our flaws, struggles, and insecurities, we wouldn't be loved or accepted.

But God already sees the real you, and He loves you completely.

God's Perspective vs. The World's Perspective

Understanding God's perspective on our identity is radically different from the world's view. The world offers a conditional, performance-based identity that is constantly changing, while God offers an identity rooted in His unchanging character and love.

Performance vs. Position

The world values identity based on achievements, status, appearance, and productivity. Acceptance is conditional, based on what you do. This mindset fuels the prototype because it teaches us that we must constantly perform to be worthy of love and belonging.

But God sees us differently. He doesn't define us by our accomplishments; He defines us by our relationship with Him. Our identity is anchored in sonship and daughtership.

As Ephesians 1:5 declares:

"He predestined us for adoption to sonship through Jesus Christ, in accordance with His pleasure and will."

Our value is fixed because it is tied to who He is, not what we do.

For years, many of us have been stuck in a cycle of performance, trying to be the perfect student, spouse, employee, or Christian. We believe that if we just do everything right, we will finally be worthy of love and acceptance. But this endless striving only leads to exhaustion and emptiness, because no amount of performance can fill the void in our hearts.

Freedom comes when we understand our position as God's children. We don't have to perform for a place in His heart; we already have one. Our worth isn't tied to titles, achievements, or how well we fit into societal expectations; it is established in who we belong to.

When we make this shift from performance to position, we can step out from behind the prototype and embrace our true, authentic identity in Christ.

Temporary vs. Eternal

The world offers an identity that is fluid and ever-changing, shaped by trends, culture, and societal expectations. What defines success, beauty, or worth today may be completely different tomorrow. This instability creates a relentless pressure to adapt and conform, reinforcing the need to present a version of ourselves that fits in.

But God offers an identity that is eternal, rooted in the unchanging truth of Scripture. In Malachi 3:6, He declares, "I the Lord do not change." Hebrews 13:8 affirms, "Jesus Christ is the same yesterday and today and forever." Unlike the world, which constantly shifts its definition of worth, God's perspective of us remains constant.

We often feel adrift, trying to keep up with evolving expectations, whether in ministry, relationships, or personal growth. But when we anchor our identity in God's unchanging truth, we find a stability that the world cannot shake. We no longer have to reshape ourselves to fit fleeting expectations because our worth is secured in something eternal.

Conditional vs. Unconditional Love

Perhaps the most profound difference between the world's perspective and God's perspective is the nature of love.

The world offers conditional love, love given when expectations are met and withdrawn when they are not. This kind of love fuels our fear of rejection, forcing us to perform in order to maintain acceptance.

But God offers unconditional love, a love that is not based on our performance or perfection. Romans 8:38-39 assures us:

"For I am convinced that neither death nor life, neither angels nor demons, neither the present nor the future, nor any powers, neither height nor depth, nor anything else in all creation, will be able to separate us from the love of God that is in Christ Jesus our Lord."

Many of us struggle to believe we can be fully known and fully loved. We fear that if God or others truly saw us, with all our flaws and failures, they wouldn't love us anymore. So we hide. Even in prayer, we wear a mask, presenting the version of ourselves we think God wants to see rather than the reality of who we are.

But in our most desperate moments, when we come to God with our raw, unfiltered emotions, we discover something life-changing: He already knew, and He loves us anyway.

This revelation breaks the hold of false identity and frees us to live authentically, because if God fully knows us and still chooses us, we no longer have to strive to be someone else.

The Biblical Foundation of Your True Identity

As you begin to shed the layers of false identity and embrace your true identity in Christ, it is essential to anchor yourself in what Scripture says about who you are. These biblical truths have been transformative in my own journey:

You Are Fully Known and Fully Loved

Psalm 139:1-4 declares:

"You have searched me, Lord, and you know me. You know when I sit and when I rise; you perceive my thoughts from afar. You discern my going out and my lying down; you are familiar with all my ways. Before a word is on my tongue, you, Lord, know it completely."

This passage dismantles the lie that we must perform to be accepted. God knows every detail about us, our thoughts, emotions, struggles, and victories, and still loves us unconditionally.

This truth challenges the belief that we have to be perfect to be loved. It frees us from the weight of performance-based identity, allowing us to step into the security of being fully known by God.

When we truly absorb the depth of Psalm 139, it becomes a powerful weapon against the fear of vulnerability. If we can't hide from God, why try? He sees beyond the layers we've built and loves us anyway.

This gives us the courage to bring our authentic selves before Him, knowing that we are fully seen, fully known, and fully loved.

You Are God's Masterpiece

For we are God's handiwork, created in Christ Jesus to do good works, which God prepared in advance for us to do. (Ephesians 2:10 NIV)

This verse shatters the cycle of comparison and inadequacy. We are not copies of anyone else; we are God's masterpieces, uniquely designed with purpose. We don't have to mimic others or strive to be someone we're not. We are already exactly who God created us to be.

For years, I felt the pressure to mirror others, adjusting my personality to fit in or striving to be the "perfect" Christian. But this truth freed me from the trap of comparison and has given me the confidence to walk in my unique identity and calling. It has been transformative, reminding me that my purpose is not found in imitation but in the intentional way God designed me.

You Are a New Creation

2 Corinthians 5:17 declares,

"Therefore, if anyone is in Christ, the new creation has come: The old has gone, the new is here!"

This powerful statement breaks the weight of past identities and false narratives. In Christ, we are no longer defined by past mistakes, failures, or rejections. We are new creations, with a new identity and a new purpose.

This truth destroys the power of shame and gives us permission to live in the freedom of authenticity. We are not bound by who we were; we are defined by God's love and grace.

When we embrace this reality, we are freed from the weight of our past and the shame of imperfection. We no longer have to apologize for being who God made us to be. Instead, we can step boldly into the fullness of our identity in Christ, walking in confidence and freedom.

You Are Clay in the Potter's Hands

Isaiah 64:8 beautifully illustrates our relationship with God:

"Yet you, Lord, are our Father. We are the clay, you are the potter; we are all the work of your hand."

This imagery dismantles the illusion of control and self-sufficiency. Just as clay does not dictate its form, we do not have to strive to shape ourselves into something "acceptable." We can trust God, the Master Potter, to shape us according to His perfect design.

I have learned, and am still learning, to surrender to the Potter's hands, trusting His process even when it feels uncomfortable or uncertain. This surrender brings a peace that performance never could.

When we embrace this truth, we are freed from the exhausting effort of trying to control every aspect of our identity. Instead, we rest in the assurance that God is shaping us with intention, molding us into something far greater than we could create on our own.

Breaking the Habit of Performance-Based Identity

Knowing that God sees the real you, and loves you just as you are, breaks the cycle of performance-based identity. But how do we move from understanding this truth to actually living it out in our daily lives?

Confronting the Idol of Self

At the core of our struggle with false identity is often an idol of self, a fixation on how others perceive us and a desire to earn approval through performance.

We don't always recognize how much we have elevated our image and reputation until God begins stripping away our false identities. We are so consumed with how others see us that we constantly adjust our behavior to maintain their approval. But this is actually a form of self-idolatry, placing our image and others' opinions above God's truth about who we are.

As I began to surrender this idol, I found freedom to be myself without constantly monitoring how others might respond. I learned to seek God's approval above all else, knowing that His view of me is the only one that truly matters.

Embracing Authenticity with God

The first step in breaking free from performance-based identity is to embrace authenticity in our relationship with God. This means coming to Him as we are, with all our doubts, fears, and struggles, rather than trying to present a version of ourselves that we think He wants to see.

I used to filter my prayers, afraid to bring my real emotions and thoughts before God. I would present only what I thought was acceptable or spiritual, assuming that my raw, unedited feelings were unwelcome. But this dishonesty created a barrier between me and God, preventing the intimacy I longed for.

When I finally began praying honestly, bringing my doubts, anger, and fears before Him, I discovered a depth of connection I had never known. God wasn't put off by my authenticity; He welcomed it. I found that He meets us in our raw humanity with grace, tenderness, and love.

Living from God's Perspective

Living from God's perspective means allowing His truth to define our identity rather than being shaped by others' opinions or our own insecurities.

Many of us live in constant fear of rejection, allowing that fear to dictate how we present ourselves. But as we embrace God's perspective, we are freed from the need for human approval. We can finally live authentically, secure in the knowledge that our worth is unshakable in Christ.

This shift doesn't happen overnight. It is a daily choice, a battle between truth and lies. But every time we choose to align with God's perspective, we weaken the grip of false identity and step further into our true selves.

With each step, the pressure to perform begins to crumble. The version of ourselves that was shaped by fear, striving, and external expectations fades away.

And what emerges?

Our most intentional, God-designed, authentic self.

Practical Steps for Living from God's Perspective

Here are some practical steps to help you shift from living for approval to living from God's truth about your identity:

1. Identify and Acknowledge Where You're Performing

- Reflection Question: Where in your life are you striving for approval or adjusting yourself to fit expectations?
- Action Step: Journal about moments when you felt the need to perform or please others. Ask yourself: Was I seeking love, security, or acceptance? Recognizing these patterns is the first step to breaking free.

2. Confront the Idol of Self

- Performance is often rooted in self-idolatry, an attempt to control how others perceive us.
- Prayer of Repentance: Daily surrender the need for approval, inviting God to reshape your identity according to His truth.

3. Seek Authenticity in Your Relationship with God

- Come before God without filters or pretense, bringing your raw emotions, doubts, and fears to Him.

- Scripture Reflection: Meditate on Psalm 139:1-4, where David acknowledges that God knows every thought and emotion, yet still loves him. Let this truth remind you that you are fully seen, fully known, and fully loved.

4. Replace Lies with Biblical Truths

- Lie: My worth is based on my performance or others' approval.

- Truth: "You are precious in my eyes, and honored, and I love you." (Isaiah 43:4)

- Action Step: Write down lies you've believed about yourself and replace them with God's truth. Speak these truths over yourself daily until they become your reality.

5. Cultivate Gratitude for Your Identity in Christ

- Shift from a victim mentality to a posture of gratitude for how God is shaping you.

- Action Step: Keep a gratitude journal, focusing on how God's mercy and grace have formed your identity. Reflect on the old patterns He's breaking and the new perspective He's giving you.

6. Walk in Authenticity with Others

- As you grow in authenticity with God, practice authenticity in your relationships.

- Practical Exercise: Share your journey with a trusted friend or mentor. Identify where you've struggled with people-pleasing and where you're learning to live more freely.

The Journey from Seen to Known

When you begin to live from the truth that God sees the real you, you embark on a journey from being seen to being known.

This journey requires letting go of the fear of exposure and embracing the joy of true connection, with God and with others.

I remember the terror I felt at the thought of being fully known by God. What if He saw all my flaws and rejected me? What if He confirmed all my insecurities? But as I took small steps of vulnerability with Him, something unexpected happened:

I discovered that being fully known was the path to being fully loved.

This realization transformed my relationship with God and others. I am finding myself more open, more genuine, no longer fearing rejection because my identity is secure in Christ.

The beautiful paradox is that the more we allow ourselves to be fully known by God, the more we discover who we truly are.

It is in this place of vulnerability and authenticity that we uncover our true identity, not in performance or perfection, but in being exactly who God created us to be.

Reflection & Activation

Take a moment to reflect on what you just read. You can engage with these prompts now, or return to them later as you process this chapter.

1) In what areas of your life do you find it hardest to believe that God fully sees and loves the real you? What fears arise when you think about being fully known?

2) How has your understanding of love been shaped by past relationships or experiences? Have you ever felt like you had to earn love or acceptance?

3) Reflect on Romans 8:38-39, which says that nothing can separate you from God's love. How does this truth challenge any fears you have about being seen and accepted by God?

4) Where in your life are you still striving for approval rather than resting in God's love?

5) What practical step can you take this week to remind yourself that you are already fully seen and fully loved? Consider writing out a declaration or choosing a scripture to meditate on.

Practical Exercise: Praying with Authenticity

One of the most powerful ways to embrace God's perspective on your identity is to practice authenticity in prayer. Here's a simple exercise to help you come before God without pretense.

1.) Create a Sacred Space

Find a quiet place where you won't be interrupted. Read Psalm 139:1-18 aloud, letting the truth that God already sees and knows you settle in your heart.

2.) Identify Where You've Been Wearing a Mask

Ask yourself: Where have I been holding back with God? Maybe it's a struggle you've been hiding, a doubt you're afraid to voice, or an emotion you've suppressed.

3.) Write a Raw, Unfiltered Prayer

Be completely honest about what you're feeling. Don't edit or "clean up" your words; God can handle your real emotions.

4.) Speak Your Prayer Aloud

After writing, say it out loud to God. Remind yourself: He already knows, and He still loves me.

5.) Sit in Stillness Before God

Take a few moments in silence, allowing yourself to be fully seen and known. Notice how it feels to be your unfiltered self before Him.

6.) Close with Gratitude

Thank God for His unconditional love and the freedom that comes from being fully known.

Authenticity with God is a practice that deepens over time. Be patient with yourself as you learn to bring your whole self before Him.

The more you experience being fully known and fully loved by God, the more your fear of exposure fades. The version of yourself shaped by performance and striving begins to disappear, and your true, God-designed identity begins to rise in its place.

In the next chapter, we'll explore the pressing process, how God lovingly removes false identities to reveal the masterpiece He created you to be.

CHAPTER 3

The Pressing Process

"No one pours new wine into old wineskins. Otherwise, the wine will burst the skins, and both the wine and the wineskins will be ruined. No, they pour new wine into new wineskins." — Mark 2:22

In the previous chapters, we explored what it means to recognize when we are living behind a mask and how God sees the real person underneath. Now, we come to an essential question: How does transformation actually happen? How do we move from simply recognizing our false self to living freely as the person God created us to be?

The answer lies in the pressing process. This is God's intentional work of breaking down old identities, dismantling idols, and revealing the person He designed. Just as a winemaker crushes grapes to release the juice inside, God sometimes applies pressure in our lives to bring forth what He has placed within us.

Understanding the Pressing Process

The pressing process is not simply about facing hardships. It is a refining work that strips away false identities and renews the way we see ourselves. It is a purification of our perspectives, beliefs, and even the roles we once thought we had to play.

I remember walking through a season where everything in my life seemed to be shifting. Relationships I believed were solid began to change. Opportunities I had counted on disappeared. My sense of security felt like it was slipping away. At first, I saw this pressing as rejection, assuming I had done something wrong. I wrestled with questions of worth, feeling isolated and unqualified.

Yet as I leaned into God, my perspective shifted. What felt like rejection was actually protection. What felt like loss was actually purification. God was stripping away mindsets rooted in comparison, performance, and people-pleasing, replacing them with His truth about who I am.

This is what sets pressing apart from ordinary struggles. It has a divine purpose. It does not simply make life difficult but specifically targets areas of false identity and gently but firmly breaks them down so that truth can take their place.

Idolatry: The Root of the Prototype

At the heart of the pressing process is God's loving confrontation with the idols we have built. Idolatry may seem like an outdated concept, something limited to golden statues and ancient rituals. Yet it is far more subtle and present in our lives today than we often realize.

Idolatry is anything, good or bad, that we place above God in our hearts. It is the source from which we draw identity, security, and validation.

How Idolatry Fuels the False Self

The prototype, or false self, we construct is always built on some form of idolatry. We shape versions of ourselves based on what we truly worship, whether it be success, approval, control, comfort, or relationships. When these things become the foundation of our identity, they move from being gifts to becoming gods.

First Samuel 15:23 provides a sobering truth: "For rebellion is like the sin of divination, and arrogance like the evil of idolatry." This verse reveals that when we trust our own wisdom above God's direction and cling to a self-constructed identity rather than surrendering to His design, we are operating in idolatry.

I did not realize how deeply idolatry shaped my false self until God began pressing against the very things I had built my identity around. Some of the specific idols He revealed included:

*The need for approval. I unconsciously molded myself to fit the expectations of different spaces. The validation I received, whether from ministry, the beauty industry, or friendships, became a temporary affirmation of my worth. Leaving certain roles felt devastating because I was not just losing an opportunity. I was losing an identity I had carefully constructed.

* Performance and achievement. Being known as a speaker, leader, or expert gave me a sense of purpose. Without realizing it, the work I did for God began to outweigh my intimacy with Him. I nearly sacrificed my family on the altar of ministry and business. Not because those things were wrong, but because they had become the measure of my worth.

* Self-sufficiency and control. I was wired to push forward, make things happen, and take charge. This drive often led me to trust my own abilities more than God's process. Like the Israelites who built the golden calf when they grew impatient waiting for Moses, I defaulted to controlling situations rather than trusting God's timing.

What makes these idols particularly dangerous is that they often appear as virtues. Self-reliance is praised as independence. People-pleasing is seen as kindness. Success in ministry is justified as

Kingdom work. When these pursuits become the source of our identity and security, they have crossed the line into idolatry.

The Destructive Power of Idolatry

Idols never satisfy. They create a hunger that can never be filled. They demand increasing sacrifice but deliver diminishing returns.

This is why the false self is exhausting to maintain. It is built on idols that require constant feeding but never truly fulfill.

Exodus 20:3 declares God's first commandment: "You shall have no other gods before me." This is not because God is insecure or controlling. It is because He knows that anything we place in His position will eventually break us.

Idols cannot sustain the weight of our worship. They will always collapse, and when they do, they take pieces of us with them.

The Wine-Making Metaphor

In Scripture, Jesus uses the metaphor of winemaking to illustrate spiritual transformation. This powerful image helps us understand what God is doing in the pressing process and how it relates to dismantling idolatry.

The Crushing of Grapes

Before wine can be produced, grapes must be pressed and crushed. This breaks the outer skin and releases the juice inside. Spiritually, this represents how God sometimes has to strip away the layers of false identity we've built rooted in idolatry and self-reliance so that we can walk in who we were always meant to be in Him.

The crushing process is uncomfortable and often painful. It confronts deeply ingrained beliefs, fears, and protective mechanisms. Yet it's necessary to release what God has placed within us, our gifts, our calling, our authentic voice.

During my pressing, God confronted beliefs I had carried for years, that my worth was tied to what I did, that I needed to earn love through performance, that struggles meant I was somehow inadequate. The crushing of these beliefs was painful, but it was making way for a deeper, unshakable foundation built on God's truth.

Fermentation – The Transformation Process

After pressing, grape juice undergoes fermentation: a transformation process where it becomes wine. This mirrors the spiritual transformation that occurs when we surrender to God's pressing and allow Him to replace our idols with genuine worship.

Fermentation happens in darkness and stillness. Similarly, our deepest transformation often occurs in seasons of waiting, silence, and uncertainty. It's in these hidden places that God does His most profound work.

During my fermentation season, I felt hidden and set aside. It was tempting to rush the process, to try to figure everything out and move forward in my own strength. But God was inviting me to stillness, to patient trust in His transforming work even when I couldn't see or understand it.

New Wine Requires New Wineskins

Jesus taught that new wine must be poured into new wineskins because old wineskins can't withstand the fermentation process. They are rigid and inflexible, unable to stretch with the transformation taking place.

In the same way, God cannot pour fresh identity, purpose, and calling into hearts and minds still shaped by idolatry. Old patterns of performance, perfectionism, and people-pleasing cannot contain the freedom and authenticity He desires to give us.

This is why the pressing isn't just about breaking down the old; it's about preparing us for what God is establishing. He isn't simply removing something; He is reshaping us to receive something far greater.

Recognizing God's Pressing in Your Life

How do you know if what you're experiencing is God's pressing and not just ordinary life challenges? The difference is that pressing isn't random; it's purposeful. While struggles come and go, God's pressing is intentional, strategic, and designed to refine you. It is not meant to harm you but to strip away false securities, remove idols, and bring you into alignment with His truth.

If you've felt stretched beyond your limits, as if life is pressing on every side, it may not be an attack; it may be an invitation. An invitation to surrender, to let go of self-sufficiency, and to trust God at a deeper level. Here are some key signs that God is pressing you for transformation:

1. A Pattern of Divine Disruption

Unlike ordinary struggles, God's pressing often disrupts areas where you've been operating in false security. It's not just one inconvenience or hardship; it's a recurring challenge that exposes deeply ingrained fears, beliefs, or coping mechanisms.

You may find yourself facing repeated relational conflicts that reveal a need for validation, or financial pressures that challenge your belief that worth is tied to performance. These disruptions are not punishment; they are divine interventions, shaking loose what is unstable so you can be built on a firm foundation.

2. An Invitation to Surrender and Transformation

In normal challenges, we seek relief or resolution. But in pressing seasons, God isn't just solving problems; He's shaping people. The process calls for surrender, inviting you to release control, pride, and self-reliance to embrace trust, faith, and dependence on Him.

I found myself in situations where my usual coping mechanisms (working harder, figuring things out, and trying to maintain control) no longer worked. I had to learn that pressing wasn't about striving through the storm but surrendering in the storm. Transformation required full surrender, a letting go so that God could do the deep work within me.

3. A Season of Divine Silence or Separation

God's pressing often involves moments of isolation, not as punishment but as an opportunity to hear Him more clearly. You may feel unseen or disconnected, even when surrounded by people. This is because God sometimes removes distractions to draw you closer to Him.

The silence is not a sign of His absence; it is an invitation to deeper intimacy. When the noise of external voices fades, we learn to discern His voice like never before.

4. Revelation of Hidden Idols or False Identities

One of the clearest indicators of pressing is when God exposes what we've unknowingly placed above Him, whether it's identity in success, approval from others, or security in control.

God presses against these false securities to reveal their insufficiency. The discomfort is real, but so is the freedom that comes when those idols are removed. What He strips away is always less than what He's preparing to establish.

5. A Call to Deeper Dependency and Faith

Pressing seasons stretch you beyond self-sufficiency, forcing you to trust God in ways that comfort never could. You may feel like you have no choice but to lean on Him because your own strength, logic, and plans have fallen short.

But this is the gift of pressing: it deepens your relationship with God. What feels like loss is actually an exchange: self-reliance for divine strength, striving for surrender, fear for faith.

God's pressing isn't meant to break you; it's meant to build you. If you find yourself in a season of pressing, take heart; He is shaping you for greater purpose.

Biblical Examples of the Pressing Process

Throughout Scripture, we see how God uses pressing seasons to refine, prepare, and position His people for their calling. These stories remind us that our struggles are not wasted. They are part of a greater process designed for transformation.

Joseph – Pressed for Purpose

Joseph endured betrayal, rejection, false accusations, and imprisonment. Yet, his suffering was not random. It was divine preparation. Every painful experience stripped away the identity he had as a favored son and reshaped him into a vessel fit for leadership.

Later, when confronting his brothers, Joseph recognized the hand of God in his journey:

"You intended to harm me, but God intended it for good to accomplish what is now being done, the saving of many lives." (Genesis 50:20)

His pressing was not just about his personal journey. It was about the lives he was destined to impact.

Like Joseph, you may be facing rejection or circumstances that feel unfair. But could it be that God is using these very experiences to strip away false identities, refine your heart, and position you for something greater? The pressing is not punishment. It is preparation.

David – Pressed in the Wilderness

David was anointed as king, but before he could sit on the throne, he spent years in the wilderness running from Saul, facing rejection, and living in caves. This season of pressing wasn't a detour from his destiny. It was shaping him for it.

It was in the wilderness that David wrote some of the most raw and intimate Psalms, revealing a heart that had learned to trust God in isolation. The pressing transformed him from a shepherd boy into a king after God's own heart.

Your own wilderness season, where doors seem closed, promises feel delayed, and your calling seems distant, may actually be God's pressing process. He is refining your heart, deepening your dependence on Him, and breaking down any idols of control, certainty, or immediacy. Leadership birthed in the wilderness is leadership that lasts.

Moses – Pressed to Lead from Identity, Not Insecurity

Moses' pressing process lasted forty years in the wilderness after he fled Egypt. This season stripped away his identity as an Egyptian prince and confronted his deepest insecurities.

When God finally called him to lead, Moses resisted:

"Who am I that I should go to Pharaoh and bring the Israelites out of Egypt?" (Exodus 3:11)

But God wasn't looking for Moses' qualifications. He was revealing Moses' true identity. The pressing had prepared him to lead, not from self-sufficiency but from complete dependence on God.

If you are questioning your own calling or feeling unqualified, consider that God may be using this pressing season to shift your confidence from yourself to Him. He is breaking self-reliance so that you can lead in His strength, not your own.

Final Takeaway

In every example, the pressing was not about destruction. It was about transformation. Joseph's trials shaped him for leadership. David's wilderness refined his heart. Moses' exile stripped away insecurity so he could lead from identity.

If you are in a pressing season, take heart. God is not just taking something from you. He is forming something in you. Trust the process, because on the other side of pressing is purpose.

Identifying the Idols That Fuel Your Prototype

Before we can fully embrace God's pressing process, we must confront the idols that have been fueling our false self. Here are five practical questions to help you uncover the idols that may be maintaining your prototype:

Breaking Free from Idolatry: Five Key Areas to Examine

1. Identify What You Worship

- What dominates your thoughts, worries, or ambitions?
- If taken away, what would make you feel lost?
- Do achievements, relationships, or status validate you more than your relationship with God?

Our greatest fears often reveal our idols. If failure terrifies you more than disobeying God, success may be an idol. If losing a relationship feels unbearable, that person may have taken God's place in your heart.

2. Recognize the False Self

- Have you shaped a version of yourself to be more accepted or admired?
- Do you adjust your personality based on who you're around?
- Are you performing instead of living authentically?

If you constantly shift to fit expectations, you may be upholding a version of yourself built on idolatry rather than true identity. God calls you to be, not perform.

3. Identify Where You're Seeking Control

- What areas of your life are hardest to surrender to God?
- Are you holding onto something just because you fear what's next?

- Are your choices driven by faith or fear?

The golden calf wasn't just about worship; it was about fear and impatience. Idols are often built when we crave certainty more than we trust God's timing.

4. Notice What's Draining You

- Are you exhausted from trying to "keep up"?
- Do you live in peace, or are you always striving?
- Are you clinging to something God has already told you to release?

Idols demand sacrifice; they drain your peace, time, and emotional well-being. If something is constantly depleting you, ask yourself: Am I carrying this in my own strength, or is this something God has truly called me to?

5. Identify the Lies You've Believed

- What belief has kept you bound to this idol?
- Do you think your worth depends on productivity, success, or relevance?
- Are you afraid that without this idol, you'll be insignificant?

The prototype is built on lies:

"I have to be perfect to be loved."

"If I stop performing, I'll be forgotten."

"I can't trust anyone but myself."

These false narratives must be replaced with God's truth.

Freedom begins with recognition. What God reveals, He is ready to heal. If He's exposing an idol in your life, it's not to shame you; it's to free you.

Responding to the Pressing with Surrender, Not Resistance

Our natural response to pressure is often resistance. We try to maintain control, avoid discomfort, or escape the pressure altogether, but resistance only prolongs the process. Surrender doesn't always make the journey faster, but it does align us with God's way, where true transformation happens.

Responding to God's Pressing with Surrender

When you recognize that you are in a pressing season, your response can either prolong the process or allow God to shape you through it. Resistance leads to frustration, but surrender opens the door to transformation. Here are five ways to respond with surrender instead of resistance.

1. Recognize the Purpose Behind the Pressing

Pressing is not punishment. It is preparation. It breaks down false identities and uproots idols so that God can establish what is true and lasting.

Instead of asking, "Why is this happening to me?" shift your perspective to, "What is God producing in me through this?" This change in focus turns pain into refining and confusion into revelation.

2. Lean Into God Instead of Pulling Away

Pressing is an invitation to intimacy. Instead of withdrawing, run to God through prayer, worship, and honest conversation.

Journaling can be especially helpful during pressing seasons. Writing out your thoughts, fears, and prayers brings clarity and helps you recognize God's faithfulness over time. Looking back, you may see how He was working in ways you could not understand in the moment.

3. Surrender Control and Expectations

Pressing requires surrendering control over the outcome, timing, and methods. It is a call to trust God's wisdom above your own understanding.

A simple yet powerful prayer of surrender might be: "Lord, I release my expectations and trust Your process. Shape me according to Your purpose, even when I do not understand Your methods."

4. Surround Yourself with Godly Community

Pressing seasons can feel isolating, but you are not meant to walk through them alone. Surround yourself with trusted, spiritually mature people who can encourage you, speak wisdom, and help you see beyond your current circumstances.

Be discerning about whose voices you allow in during this season. Not everyone will understand the pressing process or give godly counsel. Seek those who have walked through similar refining and can offer wisdom rooted in experience and faith.

5. Anchor Yourself in God's Word

God's Word provides stability in seasons of pressing. Anchor yourself in Scriptures that remind you of His faithfulness and purpose.

Romans 8:28 assures us, "And we know that in all things God works for the good of those who love him, who have been called according to his purpose."

James 1:2-4 reminds us, "Consider it pure joy, my brothers and sisters, whenever you face trials of many kinds, because you know that the testing of your faith produces perseverance. Let perseverance finish its work so that you may be mature and complete, not lacking anything."

Breaking Free from Idolatry and the False Self

Recognizing the idols fueling your false self is only the first step. True freedom requires intentional action. Here is a roadmap for dismantling them:

1. Repent and Renounce the Idols

Breaking free from idolatry begins with repentance. This is not just about feeling sorry; it is about changing direction.

Psalm 139:23-24 offers a powerful prayer for self-examination:

"Search me, God, and know my heart. Test me and know my anxious thoughts. See if there is any offensive way in me and lead me in the way everlasting."

Ask God to reveal any idols in your heart. Name them specifically and repent for placing them above Him. Declare that your identity, worth, and security come from God alone.

2. Allow God to Reshape Your Identity

After repentance comes renewal. Identity is not something you create; it is something you receive from God.

Jeremiah 1:5 reminds us, "Before I formed you in the womb, I knew you. Before you were born, I set you apart."

Ask God to show you who He created you to be beyond the masks and roles you have adopted. Surrender your self-perception to His truth.

3. Step Into Radical Obedience

Breaking free from idolatry often requires action. Faith is demonstrated through obedience.

For me, this meant walking away from a prestigious position that had become part of my identity. It meant taking time off social media to break the addiction to validation. It meant setting boundaries in relationships where I had made people's approval an idol.

What step of obedience is God asking of you? It may be releasing a title, setting a boundary, or stepping into something new that requires faith.

1 Samuel 15:22 reminds us, "To obey is better than sacrifice." Obedience is the key to lasting freedom.

4. Replace Lies with Truth

The false self is built on lies. Breaking free requires intentionally replacing them with God's truth.

Romans 12:2 instructs, "Do not conform to the pattern of this world, but be transformed by the renewing of your mind."

Identify the specific lies that have shaped your false self. Find Scriptures that contradict them and declare them over your life daily.

5. Replace Idolatry with Intimacy

Idolatry is ultimately a misplaced longing for intimacy, security, and significance. The only true replacement is a deeper relationship with God.

Jesus said in Matthew 6:33, "Seek first his kingdom and his righteousness, and all these things will be given to you as well."

Spending time in God's presence is not about religious obligation. It is about experiencing His love so deeply that idols lose their power.

The Freedom That Awaits You

On the other side of pressing, there is a freedom and clarity that can only come through surrender. It is freedom from false identities, lies, and the exhausting need to prove yourself. It is the clarity of knowing who you are in Christ, rooted, grounded, and unshaken.

Breaking Through the Lies

Lie: Struggles mean inadequacy**

I once believed that struggles were proof that I was failing. God revealed that struggles are not rejection; they are refinement. James 1:2-3 reminds us that testing produces perseverance.

Lie: I have to do everything for God**

For years, I believed that my value came from what I did for God. The pressing revealed that I was a daughter first, not a worker. Ephesians 2:10 affirms that I am God's masterpiece, created for good works, not defined by them.

Lie: Self-reliance is safer than dependence on God**

I often relied on my own strength while putting God's name on my plans. Pressing seasons exposed this false security and led me into true trust. Proverbs 3:5-6 taught me that surrender is not weakness but freedom.

Embracing Your Pressing Season

If you are in a pressing season, know this:

God is not punishing you. He is preparing you.

He is not rejecting you. He is refining you.

He is not breaking you down. He is breaking you open.

Just as a winemaker crushes grapes not to destroy them but to release what is inside, God is pressing you to bring out the beauty He has placed within you.

Surrender to the process. Trust the wisdom of the One shaping you. On the other side of pressing is a freedom you have never known, the freedom to be fully who God created you to be.

Reflection & Activation

Take a moment to reflect on what you just read. You can engage with these prompts now, or return to them later as you process this chapter.

1) What lies have you believed about your identity that contradict what God says about you?

2) Where in your life have you been living according to a false identity rather than the truth of who God created you to be?

3) Reflect on Ephesians 1:5, which says, "He predestined us for adoption to sonship through Jesus Christ, in accordance with his pleasure and will." How does knowing that God chose you challenge the false narratives you've accepted about yourself?

4) What is one truth you need to begin declaring over yourself daily to replace a lie you've believed?

Practical Exercise: Breaking Agreement with False Identity

In John 8:32, Jesus said:

"Then you will know the truth, and the truth will set you free."

This week, take intentional steps to break agreement with false identities.

1.) Write down the biggest lie you have believed about yourself.

2.) Find a scripture that directly contradicts that lie. (For example, if you've believed "I am not enough," replace it with 2 Corinthians 12:9, which says, "My grace is sufficient for you, for my power is made perfect in weakness.")

3.) Declare the truth aloud daily. Speak the scripture over yourself and pray, asking God to renew your mind in this area.

Pressing is temporary. The transformation it produces is eternal. As you surrender to God's process, trust that He is making something beautiful out of the pressing.

CHAPTER 4

Sonship vs. Orphan Mentality Stepping Into Your True Identity

The Shift From Striving to Belonging

For so long, I lived as if I had to earn my place, prove my worth, and secure my belonging. I didn't realize it at the time, but I was walking through life as if I were spiritually fatherless.

Even after knowing God, I was still grasping for validation through people, achievements, and the roles I played. I had faith, but I didn't have security. I believed in God, but I wasn't convinced that I was truly His daughter.

This is the orphan spirit at work. If you've ever felt unseen, like you have to strive to be enough, or like God's love is something you have to earn, then you may have unknowingly been operating as an orphan rather than as a child of God.

This chapter is about exposing the difference between living as an orphan and living as a son or daughter so that you can fully step into the freedom and security that already belongs to you.

What Is the Orphan Mentality?

The orphan mentality is not about whether or not you have parents. It is about how you see yourself in relation to God. It is a mindset rooted in lack, rejection, and self-reliance. It makes you believe:

- You are alone and must take care of yourself.

- You have to prove your worth through work and performance.
- You have to fight for love, belonging, and security.
- God is distant, or His promises don't apply to you.

Orphan thinking keeps you striving instead of resting, fighting for approval instead of receiving love, and controlling instead of trusting.

But here's the truth. God never called you to be an orphan.

Romans 8:15 says:

"The Spirit you received does not make you slaves, so that you live in fear again. Rather, the Spirit you received brought about your adoption to sonship. And by Him we cry, 'Abba, Father.'"

You were never meant to hustle for belonging. You already have a Father.

Signs You Are Living with an Orphan Spirit

How do you know if you are living from an orphan mindset instead of from your true identity as a son or daughter? Here are a few signs:

1. You feel like you have to earn love and acceptance.

- Orphans think they have to work harder to prove their worth.
- Sons and daughters receive love freely.

2. You struggle to trust God with the details of your life.

- Orphans believe they are on their own.
- Sons and daughters know they are taken care of.

3. You fear rejection and abandonment.

- Orphans believe love is conditional and can be taken away.
- Sons and daughters know their place in God's family is secure.

4. You compare yourself to others and feel like you're always behind.

- Orphans compete for approval.
- Sons and daughters know there is enough room for everyone at the table.

5. You struggle with rest.

- Orphans are always striving to make things happen.
- Sons and daughters know they can trust their Father's timing.

How Waiting Exposed the Orphan Mentality in Me

I never knew how much I had wrapped my identity, security, and sense of belonging around a relationship until it was suddenly stripped away.

For years, I saw myself as a daughter to this family, not by blood but by heart and connection. Their love and acceptance felt like a safe place, a covering, a deep sense of belonging that I had longed for. I had built my world around it, and in many ways, I became whatever I needed to be to stay there.

I didn't realize it at the time, but I was operating out of an orphan mentality, constantly adjusting, striving, and suppressing parts of myself in an attempt to secure my place, even though no one had actually required that of me.

When the relationship broke, I felt my heart physically shatter. Even though it was necessary for what God was doing in me, it didn't make the pain any less real.

The pain was so deep that grieving it felt like grieving a death. I wasn't just losing a relationship. I was losing a version of myself that had been built around it.

I remember begging, bargaining, and being willing to change, whatever it took, to keep the relationship intact. I was willing to sacrifice my own needs, my own voice, my own self-awareness, to avoid the deep fear that I had lost my place.

I didn't know who I was without them.

The weight of that realization crushed me.

It exposed the deep void in me, one that had been covered up by belonging to people instead of belonging to God.

I thought I was just grieving the relationship, but I was really grieving who I had been in it.

Healing and Restoration: What I Didn't Expect

I wish I could say the healing process was fast, but it wasn't.

I cried for months. Some days, I thought I was okay. Other days, I was drowning.

I went into protection mode, afraid to rebuild relationships, afraid to trust again.

But what I didn't see at the time was that God wasn't trying to steal something from me. He was trying to restore me.

And the most beautiful thing?

He did restore the relationship.

Not in the same way. Not in a way that put my identity back in it.

But in a way that honored Him first.

Now, I walk in that relationship with freedom, not fear.

I can love, but I don't need them to validate my belonging.

I can honor, but I don't have to become something I'm not to keep my place.

This is what true sonship does. It frees you from the fear of losing people because your place in God is already secure.

Final Takeaway: You Are Already Home

The orphan spirit says:

- "You have to fight for a place."
- "If you don't work for it, you don't deserve it."
- "You are not enough."

But God says:

- "You are already Mine."
- "You don't have to earn what I've freely given."
- "You have always belonged."

You don't have to fight for love, prove your worth, or strive for belonging.

You are already a son.

You are already a daughter.

And nothing can change that.

Reflection and Activation

Journal Prompt:

- Where in my life have I been living like an orphan instead of a child of God?
- What fears have surfaced in my waiting season?
- What relationships or identities have I relied on more than God?

Declaration:

"I renounce the orphan spirit and fully embrace my identity as a child of God. I do not have to strive. I am already chosen, already loved, already secure. My Father sees me, knows me, and delights in me."

Prayer of Sonship:

"Father, I repent for every place where I have lived as if I were not Yours. I renounce fear, striving, and self-reliance. I receive Your love fully. I surrender my need to prove myself. I trust You. Teach me how to walk as Your child, fully loved, fully seen, and fully secure in You. Amen."

CHAPTER 5

Becoming Rooted—Living As A Son/Daughter In Everyday Life

The Process of Becoming Established

Being rooted in God isn't just a concept. It's a process, a transformation, and a decision we make daily.

For years, I thought freedom was just about getting delivered from something. Breaking free from cycles, strongholds, or mindsets. But I learned the hard way that freedom isn't just about what you break free from. It's about what you become planted in.

If you don't establish your identity in truth, your struggles will always find a way back to you.

I spent years getting prayer after prayer, breakthrough after breakthrough, but always finding myself back in the same cycles of insecurity, striving, and fear. Why? Because I didn't know how to stay in the place of healing long enough for transformation to take root.

If we don't take time to anchor ourselves in truth, we will always feel like we are on the verge of losing what God has given us. God never meant for our freedom to feel fragile.

When you are truly planted in truth, nothing can uproot you.

Why So Many People Struggle to Stay Established in Identity

Many believers experience a powerful moment with God, whether it's a revelation of His love, a deep healing, or a personal deliverance. Then life happens, and they slowly drift back into old patterns.

It's not that the freedom wasn't real. It's that freedom has to be reinforced.

For years, I would go through cycles of getting free, feeling strong in my identity, then slowly sliding back into old struggles. I didn't recognize that when God removes something from your life, it creates space, and if you don't fill that space with truth, the enemy will try to fill it with lies again.

Freedom is not about avoiding the battle. It's about standing firm in truth no matter what the battle looks like.

Healing Has to Go All the Way to the Root

For years, I lived with constant headaches and migraines. My solution? Excedrin. Anytime I felt the pain coming, I reached for temporary relief.

I never stopped to ask: Why is this happening?

Eventually, I realized my body wasn't processing sugar well. I was deficient in magnesium and wasn't drinking enough water. The pain wasn't the problem. The root cause was.

This is exactly how many people treat their spiritual struggles.

We pray, cry, get hands laid on us, and feel better for a moment, but then the same battles return because we never got to the root.

God doesn't just want to remove the pain. He wants to deal with the source.

The real work of healing happens when you stop treating symptoms and start confronting the cause.

The Danger of Stopping the Process Too Soon

I once had strep throat and was given antibiotics to take twice a day for ten days. By day three, I felt completely fine. My throat didn't hurt anymore, and my energy was back.

So I stopped taking the antibiotics.

What I didn't realize was that just because I felt better didn't mean the infection was completely gone. Within a few weeks, my symptoms came back even worse because I had never finished the full treatment.

This is what happens when we leave the process of healing before it's complete.

A lot of people walk away from God's refining process too soon. They feel better, so they stop digging deeper. They stop pressing into truth. They stop pursuing healing.

And then the old struggles come back even stronger.

True freedom requires staying planted long enough for God to complete the process.

Choosing Where You Are Planted

Everything in your life is rooted in something.

If your identity is not grounded in God, it will find something else to attach itself to—success, approval, relationships, past trauma, performance, or fear.

A tree cannot plant itself in two different places at the same time. It must choose where its roots will grow.

When your identity is truly planted in Christ, nothing else gets to define you.

Being established in truth means that no rejection, failure, or disappointment can shake you. Your foundation isn't based on circumstances. It's based on who God is.

Reflection & Activation: Becoming Unshakable

Take a moment to reflect on what you just read. You can engage with these prompts now or return to them later as you process this chapter.

Reflection Questions

How did Jesus stay rooted in His identity? Find a passage in the Gospels where Jesus displayed an unshakable identity. What can you learn from His example?

What storms have tried to shake your identity in the past? Have you been uprooted by fear, rejection, or insecurity? How have you responded?

Imagine yourself fully grounded in Christ. If you were deeply rooted in truth, what would a day in your life look like? How would your thoughts, actions, and responses be different from today?

Practical Exercise: Standing Firm in Truth

📌 Jeremiah 17:7-8 says:

"But blessed is the one who trusts in the Lord, whose confidence is in Him. They will be like a tree planted by the water that sends out its roots by the stream. It does not fear when heat comes; its leaves are always green. It has no worries in a year of drought and never fails to bear fruit."

Imagine yourself as a tree planted by the water.

Write down one "storm" that has shaken your confidence in the past.

Find a scripture that contradicts that instability and speaks to God's truth about you.

Declare this truth aloud daily:

"I am unshaken because I am planted in Christ. No fear, no failure, and no rejection can uproot me. I am deeply rooted in truth, and I will stand firm."

As we move into Chapter 6, we will go even deeper into breaking agreement with falsehoods and reinforcing truth.

CHAPTER 6

Breaking Free & Walking In Authority

When Lies Become Reality

I spent most of my life believing a lie.

It wasn't one I consciously chose, and it wasn't one that someone explicitly told me. It was the kind of lie that seeps into your soul when love feels conditional. When rejection becomes a cycle. When you don't know where you belong.

The lie whispered through my childhood, into my teenage years, and deep into my adulthood:

"You are not enough."

I didn't say it out loud, but I lived as if it were true. I carried it in the way I approached relationships, in the way I sought approval, and in the way I shrank myself to fit into spaces where I hoped I would finally feel chosen.

But the moment I realized that lie had power over me was the moment it almost took my life.

The Breaking Point

I was never the child who felt like she fit in. I wasn't carefree or lighthearted. I carried things heavier than I should have, burdened by realities I didn't know how to process.

I grew up watching people leave. My biological father was inconsistent at best, showing up just long enough to make promises he wouldn't keep. I can still remember sitting on the sidewalk with my packed bags, waiting for him to come pick me up. The waiting always ended in disappointment.

The only person who ever made me feel truly safe was my big mama, my father's mother. She was my anchor, my steady place. She made me feel seen in a world where I often felt invisible.

And then, she was gone.

It was Mother's Day weekend of my sophomore year in high school. She had taken a trip to Houston, and I desperately wanted to go with her, but I didn't. A part of me feared the guilt of not spending the holiday with my biological mom, so I stayed.

She never made it back home.

The car accident took her instantly. One moment, she was here. The next, she wasn't.

That was the first time I felt the full weight of loss.

But it wasn't just grief that crushed me—it was the realization that the one person who made me feel loved without conditions was no longer here. I felt untethered, like I had lost the only proof that I was worthy of being chosen.

The Lie That Almost Killed Me

The weeks that followed blurred together. I cried constantly. The sadness felt unbearable, but the deeper pain was the thought:

"What is left for me?"

I had been fighting to belong my entire life. Fighting to be wanted. Fighting to be loved in a way that didn't feel like I had to earn it.

And I was tired.

I don't remember how many pills I swallowed that night. I just remember taking them.

The next thing I knew, I was on the floor of a dirty restaurant bathroom, barely conscious. My manager found me.

I can still hear her voice. She wasn't someone I particularly liked, and no one in our workplace did either. She was sharp, always demanding, rarely kind. But in that moment, she was the first person to look me in the eyes and speak life into me.

I don't remember her exact words, but I remember feeling something shift.

I should have died that night. But instead, I walked out of that restaurant with a pink T.D. Jakes Bible she had given me. That Bible became my lifeline.

I didn't realize it then, but God was rewriting my story.

When Lies Become Strongholds

Lies don't start as strongholds. They start as whispers.

One wound, one rejection, one painful experience plants a thought:

"You are not enough."

And if you don't uproot it, it grows.

Over time, it becomes a belief that shapes how you see yourself. Then it becomes the filter through which you experience life. Eventually, it dictates your decisions, your relationships, and your ability to receive love.

📖 Proverbs 23:7 says, "As a man thinks in his heart, so is he."

That is why the enemy fights for your mind. He knows that if he can get you to believe a lie long enough, you will start living as if it's true.

Recognizing When Lies Sneak Back In

Freedom isn't just about breaking the chains, it's about making sure they never return.

Lies don't always leave quietly. Even after you break agreement with them, the enemy will try to reintroduce them in moments of vulnerability. This is why renewing the mind is not a one-time event

—it is an ongoing process.

If you don't actively fill your mind with truth, the enemy will try to reclaim what was lost.

When you hear an old lie whispering, reject it immediately. Lies are like seeds, if you don't uproot them, they will take root again.

Building Your Anchor Journal

Romans 12:2 says, "Be transformed by the renewing of your mind."

An Anchor Journal is a personal tool to:

- Write down every lie you've believed about yourself.
- Find and write a scripture that contradicts it.
- Speak these scriptures over yourself daily.

This is not just about reading the Bible—it is about making truth a part of your identity.

I Come Out of Agreement / I Come Into Agreement

These statements are a starting point. As you go through your own journey, allow the Holy Spirit to reveal specific lies that need to be broken and truths that need to be established.

I come out of agreement with:

- The lie that I am unworthy of love.
- The lie that my past defines me.
- The lie that I have to perform for approval.
- The lie that I will always struggle with this.
- The lie that God is distant and uninterested in my life.

I come into agreement with:

- The truth that I am fully known and fully loved by God (Psalm 139:1-4).
- The truth that I am chosen, not forsaken (Ephesians 1:4).
- The truth that I am no longer a slave to fear (Romans 8:15).
- The truth that whom the Son sets free is free indeed (John 8:36).

Declare these over your life daily. Write them down. Make them a part of your Anchor Journal.

Final Declaration: Walking in Freedom

Isaiah 61:1 says, "He has sent me to bind up the brokenhearted, to proclaim freedom for the captives and release from darkness for the prisoners."

Today, you declare your freedom.

Speak this out loud:

"I break every lie that has kept me bound. I come out of agreement with every false belief and step into the truth of who I am in Christ. I am not my past. I am not my failures. I am not what people have said about me. I am free, and I will walk in that freedom every single day."

CHAPTER 7

Living Free & Walking In Authority

The Battle Doesn't Stop After Deliverance

Breaking free is not the finish line. It is the beginning of learning how to walk in sustained freedom. Many people believe that once they experience deliverance, they will no longer face the same battles. They assume the thoughts that once tormented them will vanish completely, that old temptations will no longer have any power, and that the struggle will simply cease.

Then reality sets in.

The thoughts still come. Temptations still arise. Old mindsets try to creep back in. It's in this moment that many people question whether their deliverance was even real. The enemy wastes no time planting doubt, whispering, "Nothing actually changed."

But the truth is, warfare often intensifies after breakthrough. When you shift from being bound to being free, the enemy sees you as a threat. You are no longer passive. You are dangerous. And he will do whatever he can to pull you back into the strongholds that once enslaved you.

Jesus Himself faced this immediately after His baptism. The moment He stepped into public ministry, the enemy came for His identity, tempting Him in the wilderness with the words, "If you are the Son of God…" The attack wasn't random. It was a direct challenge to who Jesus was.

The enemy does the same to us. His goal is not just to make us stumble — it is to make us doubt that we are free in the first place.

The question is not whether the attacks will come. The question is, will you stand your ground?

Recognizing the Enemy's Strategy

The greatest deception of spiritual warfare is that many believers do not even realize they are in a battle. They assume the heaviness they feel is just a mood. They accept anxiety and self-doubt as their personality. They explain away destructive cycles as bad habits rather than spiritual oppression.

The enemy is strategic. He is not sloppy in his attacks. He studies patterns. He exploits weaknesses. He watches how you respond to life's pressures and carefully plants seeds of deception where you are most vulnerable.

His tactics are often subtle, which makes them even more dangerous.

- He uses familiar thoughts — whispering the same lies you have believed for years.
- He weaponizes your past — reminding you of every failure, every mistake, and every place where you once fell short.
- He makes compromise look harmless — convincing you that small lapses in discipline or obedience do not matter.
- He isolates you — leading you to believe that no one else struggles like you do, so you stay silent.

Understanding his strategy is the first step in stopping the cycle. The moment you recognize that certain struggles intensify when you are pressing into God, you begin to see them for what they are—not just circumstances, but warfare.

Fighting with Truth: Spiritual Warfare in Everyday Life

For years, I thought spiritual warfare was something dramatic—casting out demons, breaking curses, fighting unseen forces. But I have learned that the greatest battles are not fought in public displays of power but in the daily decisions we make about what we believe.

Warfare is not just about fighting demonic manifestations. It is about truth confronting lies.

Jesus showed us how to fight in the wilderness when He responded to every attack from the enemy with the words, "It is written." He did not argue. He did not reason with Satan. He declared truth.

We must do the same.

When the enemy tells you, "You will always struggle with this," your response is not, "I hope I don't." Your response is, "It is written—whom the Son sets free is free indeed."

When he tells you, "You are unworthy," your response is not, "Maybe I am." Your response is, "It is written—I am fearfully and wonderfully made."

Warfare is not passive. It requires you to be an active participant in enforcing the freedom that Christ already purchased for you.

Weapons of Warfare: How to Stay Free

Staying free is not a matter of willpower. It is a matter of strategy. The same way the enemy is strategic in attacking, you must be strategic in resisting.

1. Take Dominion Over Your Thoughts

The battle always starts in the mind. Every thought must be tested against the truth of God's Word. If it does not align, it must be rejected.

"We take captive every thought to make it obedient to Christ." (2 Corinthians 10:5)

2. Guard Your Input

What you feed your mind and spirit directly impacts your ability to walk in authority. If you are consuming things that contradict God's truth—through media, conversations, or relationships—you are weakening your own defenses.

"Above all else, guard your heart, for everything you do flows from it." (Proverbs 4:23)

3. Stay in the Word

The Bible is not just a book—it is a sword. If you do not know what the Word says, you will be unarmed in battle

"Take the helmet of salvation and the sword of the Spirit, which is the word of God." (Ephesians 6:17)

4. Speak Truth Out Loud

Lies lose power when confronted with truth spoken in faith.

"The tongue has the power of life and death." (Proverbs 18:21)

5. Refuse Isolation

The enemy works in secrecy. He convinces you that your struggles are too shameful to share, keeping you trapped in cycles of bondage. Freedom is sustained in community.

"Confess your sins to each other and pray for each other so that you may be healed." (James 5:16)

6. Worship as Warfare

Worship is a weapon because it shifts the focus from the battle to the victory already won. When we exalt God, we dethrone everything else that tries to take authority in our lives.

"Let the high praises of God be in their mouth, and a two-edged sword in their hand." (Psalm 149:6)

Final Activation: Enforcing Your Freedom Daily

Write down the specific thoughts, temptations, or struggles that tend to resurface in your life. Next to each one, write the truth of God's Word that contradicts it.

Commit to declaring these truths every day for the next week.

Then, ask the Holy Spirit to reveal any hidden agreements you have made with the enemy. Are there any areas where you have accepted struggle as normal? Any places where you have unknowingly aligned with deception?

As you write, pray this:

"Lord, I break every agreement I have made with lies. I come into full alignment with Your truth. I take dominion over my thoughts, my emotions, and my identity. I refuse to live as a slave to fear, shame, or deception. I will walk in the freedom You have given me, and I will enforce that freedom daily. In Jesus' name, amen."

CHAPTER 8

Walking In Purpose, Living From Your True Identity

The Shift from Surviving to Thriving

For so long, you have fought to be free. You have wrestled, broken agreements, confronted strongholds, and walked through the fire of transformation. But now, something is different.

You are no longer fighting to be free. You are free.

This is the moment where everything shifts. Up until now, your journey has been about healing, breaking cycles, and reclaiming the identity God gave you. But now? Now, it's time to live.

This is where you step into purpose, not as a destination, but as a way of life.

What Walking in Purpose Actually Means

For years, I thought purpose was something I had to chase. Something I had to figure out, define, and perfect before I could step into it.

I believed that if I could just find the one thing I was created to do, I would finally feel settled. But I've learned that purpose is not a place you arrive at. It's a life you live from.

- Purpose is not about achieving, it's about abiding.
- Purpose is not about striving, it's about surrender.

- Purpose is not found in a title or career, it's found in obedience.

Many people delay stepping into purpose because they feel unprepared. But what if purpose is simply walking in obedience to what God is asking of you today?

Jesus didn't strive for purpose. He walked in complete alignment with the Father. His calling wasn't found in titles or positions, it was found in obedience.

I do nothing on my own but speak just what the Father has taught me. (John 8:28 NIV)

If you are fully surrendered to God, you are already in your purpose.

Breaking the Fear of "What If I Get It Wrong?"

Many people stay stuck in hesitation, asking:

- What if I step into something that isn't really my calling?
- What if I mess up?
- What if I mishear God?

But here's the truth: If you are following God, He will course-correct you.

Whether you turn to the right or to the left, your ears will hear a voice behind you, saying, 'This is the way; walk in it.' (Isaiah 30:21 NIV)

Your purpose isn't a tightrope, it's a path. And if you keep moving forward in faith, God will make sure you end up where you are supposed to be.

Fear of failure has kept too many people paralyzed. But purpose is not about perfection, it's about partnership with God.

The only way to walk in your purpose is to start walking.

Purpose Flows from Sonship, Not Striving

The world teaches that purpose is something you achieve. But in the Kingdom, purpose is something you receive.

Your purpose isn't something you hustle for, it's something that naturally flows from being a son or daughter of God.

When you are rooted in identity, purpose becomes a natural outflow of who you are. You don't have to fight to be "enough." You don't have to prove your worth through what you accomplish.

You did not choose me, but I chose you and appointed you so that you might go and bear fruit—fruit that will last—and so that whatever you ask in my name the Father will give you. (John 15:16 NIV)

If you remain in Him, you will bear fruit.

Not because you hustled. Not because you forced it. But because fruit is the natural result of staying connected to the vine.

Purpose isn't about striving, it's about abiding.

What Happens When You Walk in Purpose?

1. You Stop Over-Explaining Yourself.

When you are rooted in God, you no longer seek validation from people who don't understand your calling. Jesus never defended His assignment. He simply walked in it.

2. You Become More Concerned with Obedience Than Approval.

Before, you feared what others would think. Now, you fear disobeying God more than you fear disappointing people. Purpose doesn't come without resistance, but you are now more committed to pleasing God than to being liked.

3. You Carry a Different Weight in the Spirit.

People recognize something different about you, not because you talk more, but because you carry something real. You walk with confidence, not because you have all the answers, but because you know Who is leading you.

Your transformation is evident, not just in what you say, but in how you live.

Living a Life of Purpose – Every Single Day

Purpose is not something in the future, it's how you live today.

- When you speak life into someone, you are in purpose.
- When you love your family well, you are in purpose.
- When you walk in integrity at work, you are in purpose.
- When you create, when you encourage, when you step out in faith, you are in purpose.

Purpose is not a final destination. It is a continual unfolding of who you are becoming in Christ.

For we are God's handiwork, created in Christ Jesus to do good works, which God prepared in advance for us to do. (Ephesians 2:10 NIV)

You don't have to stress about purpose. You just have to walk with God.

FINAL ACTIVATION: STEPPING INTO PURPOSE

Write a Declaration

Take a moment to declare your purpose. Not based on a career or a title, but based on who you are in Christ.

Start with:

- Because I am a child of God, I now...
- Because I am free, I will...
- Because I am walking in truth, I will not...

Let this be your foundation. Let this be what you return to when the enemy tries to plant doubt.

FINAL CHARGE: YOU WERE MADE FOR THIS

- You were not set free just to survive. You were set free to walk in purpose.
- You do not have to figure out every detail, your job is to obey God today.
- You are not waiting to be used by God, He is already using you.
- You were created for this moment.
- You were called for such a time as this.
- You were chosen to bear fruit that will last.

This is just the beginning. Step forward in faith. Walk in purpose.

CHAPTER 9

Sealing The Shift, Walking In Unbreakable Identity

The Final Threshold, No Turning Back

There is a moment in every transformation journey when you realize, deep in your soul, that you can never go back to who you used to be. You don't just know it in your mind; you feel it in your spirit. The chains have fallen. The lies have been exposed. The old version of you has been buried, and resurrection life has taken its place.

This is that moment.

This chapter isn't about learning something new, it's about solidifying everything that has already been unlocked in you.

By now, you have confronted strongholds. You have walked through deep inner healing. You have come out of agreement with lies, stepped into purpose, and learned how to walk in authority. But this is where you establish it so deeply that nothing can shake it.

You are no longer someone trying to be free, you are someone who walks in freedom.

The Lie That Tries to Pull You Back

Even after major transformation, one of the greatest tactics of the enemy is to try to convince you that your freedom isn't real or that it isn't permanent.

You might still hear whispers like:

* What if this doesn't last?

* What if you fall back into old patterns?

* What if you aren't really changed?

These thoughts will try to creep in, especially when life gets hard. But you must remember this: Freedom isn't about never being tempted again. It's about knowing who you are even when the temptation comes.

Jesus Himself was tempted after He was baptized and filled with the Spirit. But He never once questioned His identity. He didn't entertain the lies. He didn't fall into self-doubt. He simply spoke the truth and walked in it.

This is what you must do.

Your transformation is real. Your freedom is real. You are no longer bound. Now, it's time to walk as if you believe it.

Owning Your New Identity

Your old self is gone. So why would you continue living as if it still has power over you?

When God changed Abram's name to Abraham, or Saul's name to Paul, it wasn't just a name change, it was a full identity shift. They didn't live according to who they were before. They fully stepped into their new name, new identity, and new assignment.

This is what sealing the shift means. It's not just knowing that you're free, it's living in a way that proves you believe it.

How do you know the shift is sealed?

- When you no longer identify with the struggle you came out of.

- When your first instinct is to respond to life's challenges from your identity in Christ instead of your past patterns.

- When you speak about your past as a testimony rather than as an ongoing battle.

If you find yourself wavering, go back to the truth. Remind yourself who you are. Speak it out loud. The moment you own your identity fully, the enemy loses all power to make you question it.

The Final Commission, Your Life Is Not Just About You

Everything you've walked through has been for more than just your personal freedom. Your life is meant to set others free.

Your transformation is a weapon against the enemy because now you carry the authority to break chains off of others.

They triumphed over him by the blood of the Lamb and by the word of their testimony; they did not love their lives so much as to shrink from death. (Revelation 12:11 NIV)

Your testimony carries weight. Your obedience has ripple effects. Your healing is a key that will unlock healing in others.

This is why you cannot stay silent.

This is why you must walk boldly.

The final charge of this book is this: Walk in your freedom, and use it to bring others into theirs.

Key Truths to Remember from This Journey

- Your identity is not found in what you do but in who God says you are.

- Freedom is not about never struggling, it is about standing firm in truth when the battle comes.

- Your past does not define you, limit you, or have the power to hold you hostage.

- Walking in your purpose is not about striving, it is about obedience and surrender.

- You are no longer doing things for God, you are doing life with God.

- Your freedom is not fragile, and your identity is not conditional.

- Deliverance is not just about breaking free, it is about living from a new foundation.

These truths are your foundation. You must return to them every single time doubt, fear, or old thoughts try to creep in.

Final Activation: Sealing the Shift in Your Own Words

Write your final declaration as a way of sealing the shift in your spirit. This isn't just a personal note, this is a spiritual decree.

Start with:

- Because I am free, I will no longer…
- Because I am whole, I will choose to…
- Because I am a child of God, I now walk in…

Write this down. Speak it out loud. Keep it where you can see it.

When doubt comes, declare it.

When fear rises, declare it.

When the enemy tries to pull you back, stand firm in what you wrote today.

This is the final step in sealing the shift.

THE FINAL WORD

You Are No Longer in Process, You Are Positioned

This book was never just about breaking free. It was about becoming who you were always meant to be.

- You are no longer waiting to be free, you are free.

- You are no longer striving for purpose, you are walking in it.

- You are no longer bound by lies, you are standing in truth.

- And now, the charge is simple: Live as if you believe it.

- Your story is just beginning. Now go walk in everything God created you for.

Made in the USA
Monee, IL
13 August 2025

23265271R00056